"When it comes to what counts, it's not what you know, it's what you do. Don't just read this book, <u>do</u> the contents of this book."

> Chuck Hogan
> President, Sports Enhancement
> Associates, Inc.

"Dori O'Rourke brings to the attention of the golf world those learning concepts and attitudinal insights that are shaping the styles of professional people from other disciplines. Using these methods will make better players and happier participants."

> Gary Wiren
> PGA Professional
> Director of Education, PGA

I Found the Golf God

10 Secrets for Golfing Success

DORI O'ROURKE

ON TARGET
ENTERPRISES
PUBLISHING DIVISION
SACRAMENTO

Published by:

ON TARGET Publishing
P.O. Box 163438
Sacramento, CA 95816-9438
(800) 743-4-FUN

Printed and bound in the United States of America

Library of Congress Card Catalog Number: 90-92287

ISBN 0-9628854-0-1

Cover design: Marketing by Design

First Printing February 1991

12 11 10 9 8 7 6 5 4 3 2

Special thanks to W. W. Norton & Company for permission to quote from *"Alice in Wonderland,"* by Lewis Carroll © 1971 by the W. W. Norton & Company, Inc.

To *Univen,*

the universal energy in us all . . .

Trust it,
tap into it,
and you, too, can discover
the *Golf God* in you.

CONTENTS

A Letter to My Readers

Golf has been a very important part of my life since 1981. That year I took a golf class as a sports medicine requirement in my junior year of college. It was the first time I'd played, and I fell in love with the game. So much so, that my senior year I turned in my tennis scholarship to concentrate on playing golf.

After two years, I was a 3-handicap. Soon thereafter, I decided to play professionally. I was told it was an incredible accomplishment due to the length of time I'd played.

My first professional tournament, I shot a total of 20 strokes higher than my average. Something had drastically changed. I assumed that my swing must be the problem, even though it had been fine the day before.

Despite the fact that I practiced doubly hard, doing everything I was advised, my average scores continued to go up. I became so frustrated and embarrassed, I didn't want to play.

Two years after turning professional, I had a choice, either give up the game or begin an all-out search for the answers that would allow me to turn my game around.

The extensive pursuit I chose led me to the most powerful psychological and physiological learning concepts and techniques in the world.

Among many beneficial discoveries, one stood out. The golf swing <u>was</u> the problem -- but <u>not</u> how I had expected. **The *problem* was that conventional golf instruction *overemphasized swing mechanics*, while rarely recognizing the importance of understanding how each individual learns.**

In a foreword written for my manual, *ON TARGET*, Chuck Hogan, President of Sports Enhancement Associates, describes the situation perfectly:

"Golf instruction has, in the last thirty years, been incredibly slanted to the mechanical, analytical, intellectual, lineal, temporal, verbal side of the game. Every golfer has been 'tipped' into a state of mechanical freezeout. Form has so overwhelmed function that the great technician of the swing can break 90 only on the best of days. Golfers are <u>working</u> to have a technically sound swing without any real understanding of how it relates to 'playing' golf. Without the 'playing' portion, there is no satisfaction in scoring or in self-enjoyment.

What is now evolving - - - or revolving (after all, revolution is evolution beginning in R) is a return to the game of being a whole person. It is a combination of technical with behavioral, objective with subjective, practice with play, discipline with humor, perspiration with inspiration, physical with mental."

Swing mechanics are important. At the same time, the golf instruction market is loaded with information regarding *physical* swing mechanics. I decided to write a fun story that would show you how to create the golf game you want, including the *physical* swing you desire, without discussing any swing mechanics (which also makes it the perfect complement to private instruction from your LPGA or PGA professional).

The information in this book is very special to me. You'll see that many things we've been told to do in the past are counterproductive. More importantly, you will have the opportunity to learn the concepts and techniques that have helped thousands of golfers, including myself, shoot lower scores, have a better golf swing, and enjoy golf more than ever before.

Ten of the most powerful discoveries are herein and I'm happy to say that this book has the potential to help any golfer learn how to improve their golf game . . . and in the process, learn more about themselves.

I'm glad you care about yourself enough to take the time to read and use this book. I think you'll be glad you did!

Dori O'Rourke

Special Thanks

This book would not be available without the help of many special people. I am thankful to all who have contributed their knowledge, inspiration, and time to this book and my life.

Special thanks to **Chuck Hogan**, President of Sports Enhancement Associates (S.E.A.), and **Lynn Marriott**, S.E.A. Master Professional. Their extraordinary insight and evolutionary beliefs have added greatly to my life and my work.

In addition, special thanks to **Leslie Elgood, Beth Norman, Lynne Ohlson** and **Dee Reed**, without their support this book would only be real in my imagination.

Also, special thanks to:

My Family:

My parents, **Sharon O'Rourke** and **Terry O'Rourke**; my grandparents, **Bud** and **Tina Petke**; my brothers, **Bret** and **Sean O'Rourke**; my uncle, **Bruce Petke**; my aunt, **Dee Petke**; my many cousins; and my adopted grandmother, **Alex Christian**.

My Support Team and Editing Team:

John Anderson, Sheri Bates, Kent Casey, Ted Deehr, Patricia DiGiorgio, Ellen French, Lynda Frost, Jacke Green, Janie Grosman, Lynne Hutty-Ritts, Karen Jacobsen, Linda Kingsley, Sharon Liberatore, Dawneen Lorance, K.C. Neiman, Frank Nugent, Dan Poppers, Nancy Reed, Melody Reid, Jennie Smith, Lori Soper, Alice Stivanelli, Suzanne Swendiman, Mary Thompson, and **Toni Zunino.**

Neuro Linguistic Programming Experts, Psychologists, and Teachers, especially:

Richard Bandler, John Grinder and **Anthony Robbins** (Neuro-Associative Conditioning).

LPGA and PGA Tour Players:

Al Geiberger, Ben Hogan, Nancy Lopez, and **Babe Didrickson Zaharias.**

All LPGA and PGA Head Professionals and Teaching Professionals who are striving to go beyond conventional golf instruction and really make a difference in their client's lives, especially:

Bill Ogden and **Dr. Gary Wiren.**

And, last but certainly not least, special thanks to:

All of my friends and teachers not listed above who have contributed to this book (you know who you are). And to **all of my clients** whom have allowed me the privilege of working with them to increase the quality of their golf games and their lives. Their feedback has been an invaluable teacher.

PART 1:

THE SEARCH

"Something's Missing"

Monday morning. John was getting ready to go to work as usual. However, today was different. As he finished putting on his tie, he couldn't stop thinking about *yesterday*.

That *duff* into a pond on the 14th hole was the final straw. His frustration and embarrassment had reached the breaking point. He had run over to the water's edge and hurled his golf clubs into the hazard.

He revisited the memorable scene over and over in his mind. He kept seeing the splash as his clubs broke through the mirror of water, and his playing partner's faces, as they watched in astonishment.

John remembered yelling to his ball, "Fine, if you want to go for a swim, take these with you!" He shook his head as he remembered how irrational he'd been. It was hard to believe he'd felt so self-righteous at the time.

"If golf is supposed to be such fun, how come it's so frustrating?" he wondered. John had read all the recommended books and magazines, seen several top-selling videos and gone to three different golf schools. He'd spent hours and hours hitting balls on the driving range, yet still he didn't improve. He couldn't understand why the more he tried, the worse he got!

"It doesn't matter now anyway. I don't want to see another golf ball for the rest of my life!" he declared aloud.

****

John opened the car door and got in. Just thinking about the drive to work put him into a bad mood. As the Volvo approached the freeway's on-ramp he could see that traffic was backed-up, even by Monday morning standards.

As he crawled toward town, John thought about the same question he'd asked himself every day for the past few months, "What's missing in my life? . . ." He knew he had a great family, good friends, a good job, and plenty of money. Yet, he also knew something was lacking.

****

John left the car in his hard-won parking space at the company garage. His office was two or three minutes away on foot. He grabbed his coat, his briefcase full of uninspiring paperwork, and once again, locked his car without having found an answer to his question.

He hurried out onto the crowded sidewalk and opened his appointment book to see what was scheduled for the day. Within seconds, there was a **Thud!**, as John and a slender, brunette woman bumped into one another. A jumbled pile of papers from his briefcase and the woman's satchel landed on the sidewalk.

"My briefcase *would* open up," he thought, shaking his head in disgust as they each bent down to sort through the papers that had become shuffled in the collision. He was irritated, but allowed no more than a trace of it to show when he said, "Sorry, I wasn't looking."

"Don't worry about it," she replied. From her papers and books, he assumed that she was a student at the nearby university. As the woman stood up, John took a better look at her. She looked somewhat familiar. All he could do was guess however. She didn't say another word before hustling away, once again blending into the sea of rush-hour walkers.

****

As John sat at his desk, reorganizing the papers that had fallen from his briefcase, he found a copy of an unfamiliar magazine article. He assumed it must belong to the woman he'd bumped into earlier.

He glanced over the story and chuckled. It was titled, *The Man Who Changed My Life*, and was about a *Guru* of sorts. Many people traveled great distances to get his advice and listen to his views about life. He noticed that the man was going to be living in a cabin on a mountain just outside town for the next few months.

"How fitting, the Guru lives on a mountain," John remarked sarcastically. "He started to throw the paper away, then paused. Thinking he may somehow be able to return it to the woman, he set the article aside.

****

John's day progressed uneventfully except for the thoughts of the article that kept coming to mind. It was almost quitting time when he finally gave in to his thoughts, picked up the article and read it again. This time in detail.

When he finished the article he felt a strong desire to go talk with this man. Why, he had no clue. Normally he preferred to learn things on his own and was highly skeptical of people's advice. "Have I gone off the deep end?" he wondered. "I'm actually thinking about taking time to go talk to some man on a mountain." Yet, John conceded he needed help.

It didn't take him long to decide to at least find the man on the mountain. "If nothing else, I could use a good long drive," he rationalized.

Hiking the Mountain

The best John could do to locate the man's residence was to find out where to park his car and which trailhead to start following. He had told his wife and secretary that he'd be out of town on business for a couple of days and that he'd try to call. He decided it wasn't necessary to tell them the full reason for his departure.

It was a beautiful day. As John drove, he had mixed feelings. A part of him thought this was a stupid idea, and a stronger part of him knew this was the right thing to do. He needed to talk with this man.

The old John would never have driven to a mountain looking for advice. He wouldn't even have crossed the street to find it. However, the old John didn't have unanswered questions about his life either.

"So far, so good," he thought, as he easily found the place to park his car. He got out, checked his watch, locked the car and started walking.

****

John walked almost two hours before seeing the cabin at the end of a clearing. It was a small dwelling, with a brick chimney poking through the back of its shingled roof. Two stairs led to a wooden porch. On the porch was a wooden bench and a chair. It looked like something out of an old Western.

The entire scene breathed serenity and comfort. Large windows and overgrown flowerbeds suggested peace and tranquility, not the conflict and intensity John was accustomed to. It was a perfect mountain retreat.

As John lifted his arm to knock on the door, he saw the note:

> Gone
> Golfing -
>
> Be
> Back
> Soon

He laughed at the irony of it. Four hours of searching and he'd found a note about *golf*.

John paused to think about his next move. "I've come this far. I can wait a little while," he thought, not ready to start the journey back.

After twenty minutes, John reclined on the pine bench and closed his eyes. Seeing the note had triggered thoughts of his last round. As he lay there, its pictures, feelings, and sounds haunted him. "I hope he played better than I did," John sighed, "otherwise there might be *two* depressed people on this mountain."

Slowly, John's golf images were replaced by the fresh scents of flowers and the sound of the gentle breeze rustling through the cypress and pines. Eventually he was fast asleep.

****

John felt a touch on his shoulder. Startled, he opened his eyes and saw a man standing there. He wondered how long he'd slept.

"Hi, the name's McLaughlin." A broad smile crossed the man's face. "My friends call me Mac. What brings you up this way?"

John, still groggy, mumbled, "I'm here to talk with you. At least I think you're the man I want to talk to." Standing up, John began to regain more of his senses. He held out his hand to Mac. "Let me start over. It's a pleasure to meet you, my name's John. If you are the man that some people call a guru, you're the one I came to see."

Mac laughed. "I've heard that some people call me that."

Mac was not what John had expected. He was wearing a red and black warm-up suit that emphasized his great physical condition. His hair was thick and wavy. Not at all like the bald, weathered, big-bellied man he had imagined. John was a six-footer but he felt small around Mac. He wondered whether it was his height or sheer presence.

"Welcome to my home, John. I'm glad you decided to drop in while you were in the area." Mac said, smiling at his own humor. "Come inside. Can I get you anything?"

"Ice water would be great, thank you."

As John entered, he saw a kitchen area to his left with some freshly cut snapdragons on the dining table. A hallway near the table led to what John assumed was a bedroom. Ahead of him, a well-worn couch and chair faced a large fireplace. In front of the fireplace, a wooden coffee table was centered upon a beautiful rug which covered the hardwood floor. To his right, there was an antique roll-top desk with a wicker basket, close to overflowing, at its side.

By the time John turned his attention back to Mac, the smell of good coffee filled the air. While Mac got the drinks, John sat at the kitchen table. "How'd your golf game go?" John asked, wanting to strike up a conversation.

"Great, as usual."

John assumed that Mac was being sarcastic, but he couldn't tell. "Do you play?" Mac asked, as he sat down across from John.

"Not anymore," John replied, laughing a little to try to hide his self-consciousness.

Mac noted John's awkwardness. "So, what did you want to talk to me about?" Mac asked warmly, changing the subject.

"Well, something's been missing in my life . . . I'm not sure why, but I'm not as happy as I'd like . . . and I read an interesting article about you," John stammered uncomfortably. "So, here I am . . . and to tell you the truth, right now I feel a little stupid being here."

"Well, why don't you start by telling me a little about yourself?"

John told Mac a capsulized story of his life. He mainly concentrated on a description of the frustration and emptiness he'd been experiencing the last few months, and, that although he knew he was successful in most people's eyes, he felt something wasn't right.

Mac listened attentively and John could sense that he understood. When he was done, Mac asked, "Would you like me to tell you a story about what changed my life? It might help you find the answers you're looking for."

"That's what I came here for," John said, ready to hear what Mac had to say.

"Well, I grew up ordinarily enough. When I was 23 though, something unique happened. It was summertime and I was off work early so I decided to go play golf. I played through a spectacular sunset and could see a full moon rising. I assumed I was the only one still on the course.

"As I walked toward the 18th green, I thought I saw a figure standing there. At first I wondered if I was hallucinating or seeing a strange shadow caused by the light of the moon. As I moved closer to the image, I knew it was a man. I grabbed my putter . . . just in case of trouble."

"'Hello Mac,' he said.

"He seemed to know who I was, although he didn't look familiar to me. Puzzled and frightened, I asked, 'Do I know you?'

"He said, 'No, but I have been keeping an eye on you.'

"With golf club in hand, I tried to hide my nervousness and asked, 'Can I do anything for you?'

"He calmly replied, 'No, but I have something to offer you.'

"My breathing sped up as he walked toward me holding a golf club in his hands. I became more relaxed once he handed me the club. It turned out to be a putter. The whole scene was so strange that I felt I was on a hidden camera show, or perhaps I was replaying a late night movie in my head.

"I could see there was something engraved on the shaft of the club. As I began looking at it more closely, the man said, 'One, I recommend that you decide what the writings mean to you. Two, put them to use in your life. Three, share what you've learned with others.'

"That's all he said and started to walk away. I only had time to ask him one question: 'Who are you?'

"He began to laugh, 'Just call me the *Golf God*,' he said, as he walked out of sight.

"There were 10 statements engraved on the club. I sat on the grass and read them by the light of the moon. I call them *The 10 Secrets*," Mac said, walking over to his desk and picking up a sheet of paper. Mac handed John the piece of paper which he read aloud:

The 10 Secrets

Know What You Want

Believe What Supports You

Give Energy To What You Want

Feel Like You're Going to Succeed

Trust Yourself

Do What Works For You

Remember the Good Things

Make the Most of the Present

Change What You Want to Change

Have Fun

"I spent the next several years figuring out what *The 10 Secrets* meant to me and using what I'd learned. Then, once I had a solid understanding, I dedicated my life to sharing what I had discovered with others . . . people like you," Mac said with affection. "It makes me feel good that people are able to use the *Secrets* without having to put in the years that I did."

Mac could see that the sun would be setting soon. "Do you need to start back or will you stay for dinner?"

John wasn't sure what to think of all this. Mac's story had been interesting and he wanted to hear more. However, parts of it seemed unbelievable. Either way, John was intrigued enough to accept the invitation.

****

Dinner was excellent. Mac's good cooking had made John's decision to stay a lot more pleasurable.

During dinner, they discussed their backgrounds and their families at length. John also told Mac everything that led up to his decision to quit golf, including offering his clubs as fish food.

As they sat relaxing by a freshly lit fire, John asked the question that had been on his mind since Mac's earlier story. "Will you tell me more about *The 10 Secrets*?"

"I'd love to talk about them," Mac replied, adjusting his body in the chair to get more comfortable. "Using *The 10 Secrets* has changed my life."

"Where to begin? . . ." Mac paused, looking at the fire, as if for some hidden answer. He had discussed the *Secrets* hundreds of times before. And, again he felt that same enthusiasm connected with the opportunity to share this powerful information.

John's attention was completely focused on Mac. Though still skeptical, he welcomed the new ideas, knowing that what he'd been doing certainly wasn't working.

PART 2:

THE 10 SECRETS

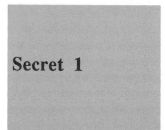

Know What You Want

Mac looked at John and said in a bold, deeper voice, "*Secret 1* is *Know What You Want*. 'What do I want?' is the first question I ask myself in any situation. Frankly, when I didn't know exactly what I wanted, I wasted a lot of time."

"How so?"

"When you don't know what you want, you do things without having a reference point. With no reference point you have no idea of whether the actions you're taking are moving you closer to, or farther away from your goal.

"Let's take the goal of happiness as an example. Before I learned the *Secrets*, I was driven to do things that I thought would make me happy. Often, I ended up following the advice of what others thought I should do.

"I went from one thing to another, hoping each would make me happy. Then I would realize they really didn't. For example, I worked very hard to make a lot of money, believing that if I had more money, I'd be happy. I pushed and pushed," Mac said, tensing his face muscles, to demonstrate the effort he'd put in.

"Finally, after doing dozens of things to become happy and still feeling unhappy, it became apparent that I could work forever toward the *idea* of happiness and never get there if I didn't know exactly where *there* was for me!

"Lewis Carroll illustrated this *Secret* in his story, *Alice in Wonderland*:

> 'Cheshire Cat,' Alice began, 'would you please tell me which way I ought to go from here?'
> 'That depends on where you want to get to,' said the Cat.
> 'I don't much care where,' said Alice.
> 'Then it doesn't matter much which way you go,' said the Cat."

"Sounds familiar," John chuckled.

"It used to be that way for me, too," Mac added. "Then, what I did that saved me years of time was to define exactly what it would be like for me to be happy. I started asking myself questions like:

* 'If I *could* have, be, or do anything I wanted, knowing that I couldn't fail, what would I want?'
* 'What is *happiness* to me?'
* 'How would my life be different if I was happy?'
* 'What is my *ideal* day like?'
* 'What is my *ideal* life like?' -- 'What does my house look like?' 'Where do I live?' 'What people are in my life?' 'What type of work do I do?'

"Two interesting things came from asking myself those questions. One, I discovered that I was closer to happiness than I had realized. And two, I created the reference points necessary to make sure that *what* I was doing was leading me toward my goals."

John smiled and confided, "You know, I've worked for over 20 years and I've never thought specifically about what I was working for. I've just been working to get ahead . . . working to be #1 . . . working to make enough money to pay the bills."

"I was the same way," Mac said. "I hadn't taken the time to decide what I wanted for a number of reasons:

1.   I always accepted what I had.
2.   I was afraid that my goals might be *unrealistic*.
3.   I was afraid of being selfish.
4.   It seemed easier not to plan.
5.   As long as I had no goals, I wouldn't fail.

"I dropped those excuses several years ago and asked myself what I truly wanted from my life. Some things I discovered were that I wanted to enjoy my work and my relationships more, get in better shape, and become a better golfer." As Mac mentioned his desire to get in better shape, John was reminded of Mac's excellent physical condition. He'd certainly achieved that goal.

"In addition," Mac continued, "I also discovered many things I didn't want. For example, I didn't want to procrastinate as much. I didn't want to be out of shape. And, I knew I didn't want to embarrass myself on the golf course."

Mac beamed as he mentioned golf. He absolutely loved the game. Since John had played, he decided to use golf for some of his examples.

"So," John said, without knowing Mac hadn't finished explaining his last comment "*Secret 1* means finding out what you *don't* want as well as knowing what you *do* want?"

"No, although I see how you could think that. Back when I thought about what I <u>didn't</u> want, I hadn't yet realized that it wasn't necessary, and sometimes even counterproductive. To know what you want all you need to do is three things:

1.   Make sure that each desire is *positively stated* in the *present* tense.
2.   State each as *specifically* as possible.
3.   *Imagine* that you already have it.

"For example, as I mentioned a minute ago, I knew I didn't want to embarrass myself on the golf course. To make this knowledge useful, I changed it to 'I am confident on every shot.' *I am confident* is **positively stated** in the **present tense**, and *on every shot* is more **specific**. Then I repeatedly imagined that I was already confident on every shot.

"Why would I want to pretend I have something that I <u>don't</u> have yet?" John asked."

"Because," Mac said, "Psychological studies show that the brain doesn't distinguish between something that is *real* and something that is *vividly imagined*. Therefore, *imagining* that you already have something you want is the quickest way to get your brain-body to make it a reality for you."

John nodded somewhat skeptically. "But, how can I *feel* confident when I know I repeatedly hit bad shots?"

"Easy," Mac grinned. "If you know that you want to feel confident before every shot, simply *pretend* that you do.

"How do I do that?" John exclaimed.

"What I do, is pretend I'm confident and experience what confidence is like with *all* of my senses. For example," Mac said, sitting up in his chair, "I imagine what I *see* when I'm confident. I *feel* what it's like to be confident. And, I *hear* what I am saying to myself and what other people are saying to me when I'm confident.

"That sounds pretty far out," John said, shaking his head.

"Well," Mac went on, "the human brain is absolutely incredible. Our brains are constantly working, moving us in the direction of our most vivid images. Our brains, being goal-achieving by design, find a way to move us in the direction of our images. If you pretend you are how you'd like to be, your brain will move you in that direction."

John wanted to clarify one point. "When you say *images*, do you mean visualizations?"

"When I say *images*, I mean images from all five senses. In addition to the visual sense, there are the senses of feel, sound, taste, and smell.

Mac got up from his chair. He reached for the coffee pot and offered John a cup. With his cup filled, John raised his cup and said, "to your health Mac."

"And to yours," Mac replied. "Now, to continue what I was saying, the brain moves us in the direction of its images whether we want it to or not. A friend once described the process like this:

> In all of nature,
> there is no such thing as
> staying the same . . .
>
> you're either striving
> to make yourself better
> or
> allowing yourself to get worse.

"To me, this is a reminder that if I don't take the time to tell my brain what I want, it will move me toward the images that are there. If I'm not already moving in the direction I want, it's a pretty good bet that the images that are there are not the ones I want to continue creating my future.

"In addition, because I believe my mind will move me toward the images I have, I've learned to be careful what I ask for. I need to be sure I really want it. "Ancient Chinese proverb says," Mac shared, in his best Charlie Chan impression, 'Be careful what you ask for because you just might get it.' Not-so-ancient Mac's proverb is 'Ask for exactly what you want and know you'll get it!'

"Just for fun, John, repeat these statements after me and see what images they bring to mind. Don't hit the ball out of bounds . . . Don't hit the ball into the sand . . . Don't hit to the hazard on the right."

As John repeated each sentence aloud, colossal images of water hazards and sand traps jumped to mind. "I see what you mean," John replied, "by trying not to think of something, I think of it."

"Precisely. The mind doesn't acknowledge the word <u>not</u>, it only sees the image you are avoiding. If you don't mind me asking, what do you think about when you're about to hit a shot?"

John answered immediately. "When I am getting ready to hit a shot, I think about things like keeping my head down, swinging slowly and following through."

"Well," Mac replied, "is swinging in a particular way what you really want? Or . . . do you really want to go to a particular target?" Mac could see that John was thinking about what he'd just said.

Mac continued. "Rather than assume that keeping your head down, swinging slowly, or following through will make the ball go to your target, why not simply imagine what you want -- the target!"

"Hmmm, that makes sense."

John looked at Mac, "So what you're saying is that on the golf course I should only think about my target so my brain will move me in that direction?"

"Exactly."

"And," John said, "when I think of swing thoughts, my golf ball won't necessarily go to my target because that's not what I'm *asking* for."

Mac gave John a quick thumbs-up, as he rose to stoke the fire.

John sat there thinking about what Mac had said. He remembered times when he went through the motions without direction, accepting mediocre results from life as if they were what he *deserved*.

"Do you have some paper I could use?" John asked.

Within seconds, Mac was back with a pen and pad of paper. John wrote a few notes:

$$
\boxed{
\begin{array}{l}
\textit{SECRET 1 —} \\[4pt]
\underline{\textit{KNOW WHAT I WANT}} \\[6pt]
\textit{1) State it positively} \\
\textit{and in the present} \\
\textit{tense.} \\[4pt]
\textit{2. Be specific.} \\[4pt]
\textit{3. Imagine that I} \\
\textit{have it NOW.}
\end{array}
}
$$

After John was done writing, Mac asked him if he had any questions about *Secret 1*.

"No, it all makes sense now."

"Great, then," Mac replied. "Let's go on to the second *Secret*. I can't wait to tell you about my experiences using it."

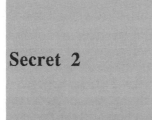

Secret 2

Believe What Supports You

"*Secret 2* is one of the most powerful *Secrets*. It is *Believe What Supports You.* Living by this Secret has had a huge impact on my life," Mac stated. "As you know, we all have beliefs about many things, including people, aging, our athletic and intellectual abilities, and so on. It is vital that we understand that **what we believe governs our lives**. We can do almost anything simply by believing we can. At the same time, whenever we believe we <u>can't</u> do something, we're always right.

"Once I watched a hypnotist who selected his subjects from people in the audience. After being placed under hypnosis, one woman couldn't say her name, and a football player couldn't lift a pencil. The *potential* to do those things still existed. It was just that that hypnotist had placed limiting beliefs into the subconscious part of their minds.

"*Secret 2* has taught me that if a belief supports me, use it. If it doesn't, change it."

"What do you mean by *support*?" John asked.

"Good question," Mac replied. "A belief *supports* me if it helps me move toward what I want. A non-supportive belief is one which limits my success. Take the first running of the four-minute mile. For hundreds of years people believed it couldn't be done. Doctors even wrote articles explaining why it was physiologically impossible. It was instilled in the minds of runners that the four-minute mile record couldn't be broken.

"Then the Englishman, Roger Bannister, *believed* it was possible, and did it in 1954. The next year 35 people broke the four-minute mile. In 1956, more than 300 people did it!

"Now let me make sure I understand," John said. "You're saying, for example, that believing you're a good golfer as opposed to believing you're a terrible golfer would be a supportive belief, right?"

"Precisely."

"But Mac, what if I *am* a terrible golfer?" John asked. Mac smiled. He could hear the depth of John's belief.

"There's a big difference between thinking you're bad at something and acknowledging that you haven't learned how to do something yet. I recommend that you believe you're good at everything you do, including golf. At the same time, know that if you choose to, you can always improve.

"The magic of *Secret 2* begins by asking yourself these questions about your beliefs:

*   Is it helpful for me to believe this?
*   Does believing this help me move toward what I want?
*   What if everything I believe comes true? Is this the future I want to create?"

Mac could see that John needed some time to mull over these new concepts. He paused for a minute and then continued. "There's always two ways to look at every situation, so why not believe what supports you? For example, people cite hundreds of reasons why golf is a difficult game to play. To name a few:

*   'You have to wait too long between shots.'
*   'There is only a small margin for error.'
*   'The golf swing is unnatural.'
*   'It's the only sport where such a long instrument hits such a tiny ball, at such a high rate of speed.'
*   'Everyone *says* it's difficult.'

"Why not look at those same things in a more helpful way?:

*   There is a lot of time between shots to relax and get ready for the next challenge.
*   You only need to do a few things *right* in order to play well.
*   The golf swing is a very natural motion, since all motion is learned.
*   Every fairway affords a huge margin for error in which to land such a tiny ball in.'
*   For every part of the game, there are some golfers who find it easy.

"I don't know whether the game of golf is *truly* easy or not." Mac continued. "What I *do* know however, is that as long as I believe that the game of golf is easy, all doors to success are open. Of course, simply believing I'm a great golfer may not make me a great golfer if my other mental and physical mechanics aren't supportive. However, it removes any limiting beliefs and allows me to tap into my full potential at that moment."

John looked at Mac. "The idea of changing beliefs that aren't supportive sounds great but it isn't an easy thing to do."

"I bet it's not for you."

When John realized what he'd said, he smiled and asked, "How can one *easily* change their beliefs?"

"The first step is to uncover your limiting beliefs. The best way I've found to do that is to get a pen and a piece of paper and to write down exactly what you want. Then, sit quietly, patiently listen to your mind and body, and list all the limiting beliefs you discover.

"For example, someone could write 'I want to shoot in the 80's by next season'. Their limiting belief list might look like:

1. I don't have enough time to practice.
2. I'm not a competitive person.
3. I started the game too late to be any good.
4. I can't hit my driver.
5. I have a lousy swing."

"That sounds like me," John responded. "I can think of several limiting beliefs my wife and I have both had. My wife is certain that she doesn't play well because she's not athletic. I believe I'm not a fast learner."

"Yes, there are an infinite number of limiting beliefs," Mac agreed. "And, happily, an even greater number of supportive ones!

"John, whenever you uncover a limiting belief, write a list of all the reasons why you need to change that belief -- why you will no longer accept that belief in your life. Make the list as long as you can. Keep on writing until you can't think of anything else to write. Once you have the feeling that your mind is ready to throw out the limiting belief, then simply substitute a more helpful belief in its place.

"Many times a limiting belief changes permanently once you become aware of it, list the reasons why it needs to change and substitute a helpful belief in its place."

"Sounds easy enough," John replied

"Great! Thinking it's easy sounds like a helpful belief to have!" Mac said, making a drum roll on the coffee table.

John reached for his pad of paper and asked Mac to continue. "Well, really John, if you don't have any questions, we have arrived at *Secret 3*."

"I can't wait," John declared, thoroughly enjoying the information he was receiving. "First though I'd like to take a couple of notes." Mac went into the kitchen as John added to his notes:

Secret 2 —

BELIEVE WHAT SUPPORTS ME

Ask myself - Is it helpful for me to believe this?

To change beliefs —

1. Uncover them
   a) WRITE what I WANT
   b) Sit quietly a few minutes and imagine that I have what I want
   c) List the limiting beliefs I UNCOVER.

2. FOR each limiting belief, list all of the REASONS why I must change — make this list as long as I CAN.

3. Substitute a helpful belief in each one's place.

Secret 3

Give Energy to What You Want

Mac plopped his coffee cup back onto the saucer and began to talk again. *"Secret 3* is, *Give Energy to What You Want,"* he said, emphasizing the word *energy.* "Knowing what you want is one thing. But, to give energy to it, you need to repeatedly imagine it exactly how you'd like it to be, and take actions directed toward achieving it."

"How does one do that?"

"One of the best ways to do this is to limit your focus to one thing at a time. It's all we can do effectively anyway," Mac said, reaching over to grab some paper. John could see him drawing something. He enjoyed watching Mac's intensity.

Mac handed the paper to John and asked, "What do you see?"

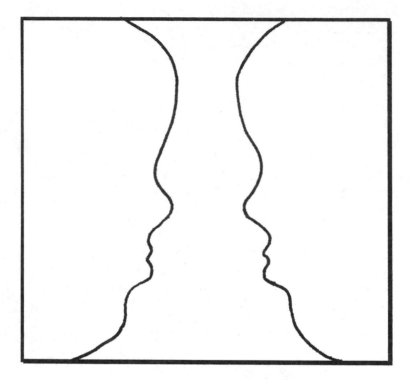

John loved a challenge and he studied the picture for a long time before answering. "I see two things depending on how I look at it. Two heads or a candlestick."

"Great," Mac responded. "Can you see both at the same time?"

John looked at the picture several times. "Sometimes it seems like I can, but neither is well-defined."

"That's how it is for most people," Mac explained. "To go from one thought, or image, to another, the brain has to switch channels -- like changing channels on a television. And, when people try to think about more than one thing at a time, what usually happens?"

"They don't get anything done effectively."

"Yes," Mac agreed. "They get caught between channels and find themselves in a *no-man's land.* Like some golfers, isn't it?" Mac said with a wink.

John nodded in acknowledgement.

Mac paused and gazed into the fire. He began to chuckle. "I used to *practice* a lot. At least that's what I called it. I'd prepare for each shot by thinking about *all* the things that I needed to do to hit the ball well. First it was my grip, then ball position, then stance, swing speed, weight shift, and head position."

"Don't forget the follow through," John said, laughing. He had recognized himself in Murphy's example.

"Golfers get so caught up in thinking about their *swing list* that they rarely focus on the outcome they truly desire," Mac said, "like hitting the ball more squarely.

"I can recollect only three golfers who knew specifically what they wanted to accomplish during their practice session. Unfortunately, the majority of golfers try to think of several things at once, think about them in an unhelpful way, and call it practice. Of course it is a kind of practice . . . practice that achieves haphazard results."

"No wonder I felt so frustrated on the practice range," John reflected. "The more balls I hit, the harder I thought about all the things I needed to do, the worse I got!"

"You've got it," Mac said. "And, there is another thing that golfers often do which moves them away from what they want." Mac stopped to make sure he had John's full attention.

"OK, tell me," John urged. "The suspense is killing me."

"They think about what they don't want. For example, how often have you thought about what you're doing wrong?"

John thought about it. "Well, I suppose I do that a lot, if you mean by focusing on my slice . . . and problems like that."

"Yes," Mac said, as he reached for another piece of paper. Mac drew a dotted line across the center of the page and labeled it, *Where you are*. Next, he drew a line toward the top of the page which he labeled, *What you want*, and a line toward the bottom of the page which he labeled, *Unwanted results*.

"Think of it as a spiral. If you want to move in this direction," Mac said, penciling a corkscrew toward the upper line, "then focus on what you want and take actions that will lead you there. If you doubt yourself, *act as if* you are there.

"If you think about what you don't want, or try to think about more than one thing at a time, this is what happens," Mac stated, while drawing a spiral down toward, *Unwanted results*.

"Are you saying," John asked, "that if I think about what I want, I will get it?" Mac could feel his skepticism.

"Not exactly. For example, if you are on the golf course thinking about your target, it doesn't mean that you'll definitely hit it there. What it does mean though is that your brain is using all of its available resources to move you in that direction.

"If you act as if you have what you want, imagining it with all of your senses, I can guarantee you that you will *spiral upward*. There's no other way the brain can go but up, up, up!" Mac said, waving his arms skyward.

"It sounds easy if I understand you correctly. All I need to do is think about what I want and take action toward it, to spiral upward to whatever I want!"

"By George . . ."

"There's just one question. Are there specific actions to take that we haven't discussed?"

"Yes, you'll learn more specific actions to take as we discuss the other *Secrets*," Mac said. "But first, how about a little stretch outside?.

"I'll be right out. I'd like to add your diagram and a few more thoughts to my notes. John added:

Secret 3 —

GIVE ENERGY TO WHAT I WANT

WHAT I WANT

↑ Imagine I have what I want.

↑ Act as if I have it

- - - - - - - - - -

WHERE I AM

↓ Thinking of more than one thing

↓ Thinking about what I don't want, i.e. what I'M doing wrong

_____

UNWANTED RESULTS

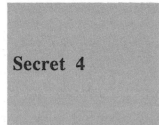

Feel Like You're Going to Succeed

The full moon was casting long shadows across the cabin porch. Above the mountaintop the stars decorated the sky like glitter. "I love it up here," John said. "It really expands how you look at life . . . changes your perspective . . . allows you to see what is really important."

"I know what you mean," Mac agreed. "Looking at the stars I sometimes see a *multitude* of spirals, all leading me toward what I want."

Mac turned to John. "Have you ever hit a golf shot that felt perfect ?"

"Sure, several that I can remember."

"Well, then all you need to do is recreate the *state of mind* you had at that time and you will hit perfect shot after perfect shot."

John looked skeptical.

"You know those times that you've heard golfers say they played 'over their head'? They were just describing a certain state of mind. I used to have the state of mind that produced the exact golf shots I wanted once or twice a year. Now, I can almost always create the optimal state of mind for great golf."

"Where do I sign-up?" John joked, wanting to believe, yet not sure it was possible.

"You can enroll as soon as you understand *Secret 4: Feel Like You're Going to Succeed.* As you know, we all have feelings: happiness, sadness, anger, peace, confidence, and so on."

John nodded.

"I divide these feelings into two groups: ones that empower me like confidence, creativity, decisiveness, serenity and centeredness; and ones that weaken me like frustration, fear, anger, confusion and tiredness.

"Tell me John, do you think you'd play a better round of golf if you were told before teeing off that you'd just gone bankrupt or that you'd won a million dollars?"

"That's pretty easy to answer."

"Of course! If you create a powerful state of mind prior to every shot, you increase your chance of success astronomically!" Mac said, rising to his feet.

"When you feel powerful, you are giving your brain a lot of good choices. When you feel powerless your brain's choices for behavior are limited."

"What kind of *choices*?" John asked.

"Well, think of your state of mind as a menu. When you feel powerful, your menu might list these choices: you will connect the ball solidly and land five yards left of your target; you will connect the ball solidly and hit a high draw; you will hit the ball low with extra distance, and so on.

"When you are in a weaker state of mind, then the menu might list these choices: top it; hit it fat; slice it; hit it short; and so on. Does that make sense?" Mac asked.

"Unfortunately, it does," John replied.

"I used to go through life accepting the state of mind that my experiences in life triggered. Since I didn't know that my state of mind could be controlled, I would show up at the golf course and accept whatever state of mind occurred for me.

"If I didn't golf well the first couple of holes, I'd start to feel anxiety or frustration. This would lead to a weaker state of mind, which lead to a complete downward spiral."

"If you want to control your state of mind, the fastest and easiest way is to change what your body is doing. This includes your facial expressions, your breathing, stance, movements, and so on. What we do with our bodies sends direct messages to our brains.

"What state of mind do you think I have now?" Mac dragged his feet as he stepped off the porch and walked slowly around with his shoulders slumped, his head drooped, and his face downcast and frowning.

"I'd say you're depressed," John answered.

"Great! What state of mind do I have now?" Mac asked. With a big smile, he pumped a clenched fist in the air, jumped off the ground and let out a great yell.

"I'd say you've just made a hole-in-one."

"Superb," Mac applauded, "What you just did was uncover how different body positions and breathing affect state of mind. To find out what my brain associates with *good* golf and *bad* golf, I simply remember past experiences."

"Will you show me what you mean?" John asked.

"Why don't *you* show me what I mean?" Mac replied, smiling, and gesturing for John to step off the porch. John looked reluctant but got up anyway.

"Now, think back to a time when you were playing poorly."

"That's easy," John said disgustedly.

"OK, now recreate the body positions and movements that you had on that day," Mac directed.

John felt self-conscious. "What do you mean?"

"I mean, walk around and *feel* what you were feeling," Mac urged. He could see that John still wasn't acting in a way that would be useful to him once he left the mountain.

"OK," Mac said. "Let me show you what I mean. When I'm playing badly I walk slowly, my shoulders slump, my head is drooped, my muscles are tight, my eyes are jumping around, my mouth is pursed, I feel heavy, and I breath shallowly and rapidly" As Mac was talking, he started breathing shallowly and rapidly and assumed his *bad* golf posture.

Then after a few moments, Mac changed his posture and breathing again. He stood tall with his shoulders back and his head up. He smiled. He breathed more deeply. He walked faster and more lightly. His eyes were centered and he looked more relaxed. "This is an example of how I am when I'm playing *good* golf."

After watching Mac, John started to have fun with the exercise. He began learning some very important distinctions between his *good* and *bad* golf positions and breathing. "Now, go from one to the next just for fun," Mac suggested.

John followed Mac's lead. "Isn't it great?" Mac said enthusiastically. Now you can quickly and easily change how you feel by just changing your body position and breathing. In a matter of seconds you can bring on a very powerful state of mind."

"That's pretty fun," John smiled, not believing earlier that he'd get much out of the exercise. "What about beginning golfers though? How would they know their breathing, body positions and movements for powerful states of mind if they've never played?"

"Well," Mac replied, "a powerful state of mind is powerful whether it's for golf or anything else. For example, let's say that you were a businessman just learning to golf. To discover powerful positions, movements and breathing for golf you could simply look for past times when you've felt confident in business situations."

"That's too easy."

"John, you've just hit upon the *hardest* thing about the Secrets -- they're easy." Mac smiled broadly. "Many people are so used to things being difficult that when something is easy, they find it hard to believe it works. On the other hand, I could make them more difficult if you'd like."

"No thanks. I'd prefer to just go inside and make a few more notes," stated John, gesturing toward the house. They walked inside. Mac went into the kitchen and John sat back down on the couch and started to write:

SECRET 4 —

FEEL LIKE I'M GOING TO SUCCEED

A powerful state of mind is the __KEY__.

The quickest way to change my state of mind is to change body positions, movements and breathing.

MY GOOD GOLF	MY BAD GOLF
Head & eyes up	Head & eyes down
Shoulders back	Shoulders slumped
Slight smile	Serious face
Breathing - easy and relaxed	Breathing - fast and shallow
Walking - even paced	Heavy steps & fast paced

When John finished writing, he said, "I'm still not sure I completely understand *Secret 4*. Are you saying that beginning golfers and golfers who don't play very well can play with confidence?"

"Definitely! Confidence isn't something that needs to be developed with experience. You don't have to wait *until* you have a good swing to have confidence. In fact, without confidence you'll have a much harder time learning a good swing. Confidence is just a feeling. You can feel it any time you want by simply changing your breathing, posture and movements.

"We are capable of doing so much more than we think we can. Rather than thinking 'I can't', or 'I don't think I know how', we simply need to pretend that we *can* and act like we know *how*.

"Pretend, pretend, pretend -- your brain will forget you're pretending and you'll start doing things that you didn't think were possible before!"

John dropped the notepad and said, "I believe it all makes sense."

"Well, alright, it's on to *Secret 5*."

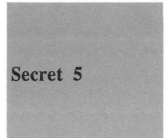

Trust Yourself

Mac was on a roll now. He lounged back in his chair and said, "*Secret 5: Trust Yourself,* is one of my favorites . . . because to me, when we trust ourselves, we trust the incredible power we have as human beings. We all have within ourselves, an energy beyond our current comprehension," Mac said, his words gaining velocity.

"To tap into our unlimited personal power, all we have to do is trust it."

After a slight hesitation, John asked, "What do you mean, exactly, by *trust?*"

"What I mean by trust is to release conscious control and let our incredible subconscious abilities take charge."

"How do you do that?"

"The answer to that question would be worth millions," Mac said slowly, "because you can't really *do it* since to try to *do* anything is acting consciously. The key is in the subtle difference between the more *passive* process of pretending and simply *noticing* what is happening, as opposed to the more *active*, conscious process of *trying to do* something.

"If you can let go of trying to make things happen, and instead, simply notice what is happening, you will learn more quickly and get better results. For example," Mac said, as he got up to stretch his legs, "there are two ways you could practice better ball contact on the driving range. One way is to *try to make* the club and ball connect. The other way is to swing and *notice* how closely the club and ball connect.

"By simply *noticing* and trusting the subconscious to take in the results and make the adjustments necessary for future success, you'll learn a lot faster. Instead of positive or negative thoughts, you are simply noticing and learning from all of it."

"So you're saying that every situation is an opportunity to learn?" John asked.

"Yes," Mac said, "but only if you let go of the conscious desire to control the situation. For example, 'Keep your head down', 'Keep your arms relaxed', and 'Shift your weight' are all conscious commands that interfere with our perfect learning system."

"But," John thought aloud, "if you don't tell yourself how to swing, how will you know you're doing it right?"

"You can answer that if you get up and start walking with me." John stood up.

"OK," Mac said, "Pretend that while you are walking, the ceiling is getting lower and lower. As you walk, you need to bend more and more so you don't hit your head on the ceiling." John followed the directions and soon was walking at about half his normal height.

"Great," Mac stated, "go ahead and walk normally again. Now, tell me exactly how much ankle flex, knee, waist, and neck bend you needed to walk when the ceiling was at its lowest point. Then, when you're done figuring that out, tell me which muscles needed to relax and which needed to contract at each moment, and to what degree."

"Very funny," John quipped. But then he thought about the question. "Are you saying that *even without telling myself what to do*, my subconscious handled the coordination of several different muscle groups -- PERFECTLY?" John asked, as he sat down.

Mac nodded. "As human beings, John, there is almost nothing we <u>can't</u> do. There are just things we have not yet learned or do now allow ourselves to learn. You have children, right?"

"Yes, I have three."

"Then you know how quickly kids learn. How do they do it? Is it a difficult process? Is it a process that requires a lot of thought? Heck no. Children learn simply by keeping their goal in mind and going for it. If they're not successful, they just do it again until they get what they want. They don't consciously tell themselves what to do . . . they just . . . what?"

"Do it," John chimed.

"Exactly. Now, picture a child learning to eat. They know their goal is to get the spoonful of food into their mouth. At first, their arm zig zags through the air, eventually landing food on their cheek or chin. Eventually, through repeated attempts, their brain is able to hone in on their target and the child learns to eat."

"Are children more capable of learning than adults?" John asked.

"Definitely not. But, by the same token, I don't believe that most adults give themselves the freedom or the time to learn. If they did, they would learn just as quickly as children. After all, aren't we all just grown-up kids?" Mac said winking.

"Now, here's an example of a golfer trying to learn to eat food." Mac said, standing to demonstrate.

"This golfer knows that the goal is to get food into his mouth. So, before trying it on his own, he bought some books to read up on how his arm should move. Right off the bat, he's forgotten his original goal, and is focusing on trying to make his arm move correctly.

"In an attempt to feed himself he plasters food on his chin and gets mad at himself, expecting to have the process perfected (since he's read about it). He bangs his spoon on the table, and wonders why he can't eat correctly. This leads him to begin wondering what is wrong with him. He starts to believe that he must be uncoordinated. When food does get into his mouth, he figures it's just a fluke. He believes that he must just be a *bad eater* and agonizes about the fact that he'll never eat as well as, let's say . . . Jack Nicklaus."

John was laughing loudly. "I know this is a bit of an exaggeration," Mac said, "but isn't this how adults try to learn golf?"

"Unfortunately, I can relate," John said, shaking his head. "But can we back up a bit? Are you saying that books aren't a good way to learn?"

"Not at all. It really depends on what you want to learn. Books are great for learning the rules and etiquette, and for explaining strategies, such as course management and club selection. In addition, they're good for learning about concepts such as ball flight, the effects of wind, different lies and so on. But books are not the best way to learn the golf swing.

"The reason is simple. It is very difficult to interpret an author's verbal directions regarding a physical motion. Furthermore, I do not believe that there is one *right* way to swing that works for everyone. Therefore, even if you could interpret an author's verbal directions correctly, their directions may not be the best ones for you.

"Remember when you were pretending there was a descending ceiling? If we had a group of people do that, we'd find that they all did it differently. Because of the varying strength and flexibility in their muscles, which muscles were used and to what degree would vary. This means that their mental picture and feeling of the motion would vary. Therefore their description would vary, and so on.

"Look at Chi Chi Rodriguez, Fuzzy Zoeller, and Nancy Lopez. Do they swing the same way? Definitely not. However, they all produce extraordinary results. The best way to learn a golf swing is to keep your energy directed specifically at what you want, and to trust your subconscious to adapt, just like babies do when they learn to eat."

"So, how would I learn how to keep from topping the ball?" John interjected.

"I recommend that you would start by forgetting your current list of golf swing *how-to's*. This means forgetting about all the things you *think* your body has to do in order to hit a golf ball. Your body does not hit the ball, your golf club does. Therefore, focus on what your clubhead needs to do to produce the result you want.

"Make it easy on yourself. If you think about the clubhead, there are only a few things it has to do correctly to hit the ball well. On the other hand, if you try to think about all the things your body needs to do to swing, you could come up with a list of over 100 things.

"I'm not saying that you can't learn to hit the ball well by thinking about your body parts. I'm suggesting that there may be an easier way. Compare it to eating. If you think about what your spoon needs to do, it's a small list. On the other hand, if you tried to think about what your fingers, wrist, arm and shoulder should do, you could get quite a list."

"Are you saying, if my problem was topping the ball, all I would need to do is go to the range and think about connecting the club and ball better, without thinking about what my body needs to do?"

"Exactly," Mac confirmed.

"It's hard for me to imagine what it would be like to be hitting balls on the range or taking a lesson without thinking about what my body needs to do."

"Well, sure," Mac agreed. "Even after I understood the extent of my personal power, a part of me still doubted whether it would work for my golf game. But I kept believing that only my subconscious truly knew what would work best for me to produce the results I wanted. And, it paid off.

"I was able to fully trust this process in my golf game once I used it and experienced it's incredible power. Speaking of producing desired results, I think it's time for me to turn in. How about picking up with the other five *Secrets* in the morning?"

"Sounds great," John agreed, rising from the sofa. It felt good to get up and stretch and it would feel even better to turn in for awhile. John's head was full and a good night's sleep might allow his brain to assimilate some of this information.

Mac brought out some blankets. As he was about to return to his bedroom, John said, "Hey, I have a great idea. Let's produce an *Eater's Journal*. It would be a magazine for people who wanted to eat better. We could interview all the best eaters in the world, and have articles discuss all the things to do in order to eat perfectly."

"Sleep well," Mac smiled, amused with John's comments. John wrote a few more notes before falling asleep:

SECRET 5 —

TRUST YOURSELF

<u>Trying</u> to make things happen <u>interferes</u> with my subconscious

To achieve anything I want, I simply need to trust myself.

To do that, I just need to keep in mind what I want and <u>notice</u> what is happening.

FOR GOLF

Swing the clubhead (don't think of the how-to's), let my subconscious make the changes necessary in my body.

The only "right" way to swing is the one that is <u>RIGHT</u> for me.

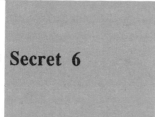

Secret 6

Do What Works For You

When John awoke, it took him a few seconds to remember where he was. Since he was sleeping on an unfamiliar couch, it was apparent that last night wasn't a dream. He could see the sun shining in the window and figured it must be later than his usual wake up time of 6:00 am.

He sat up, reached for his watch, and looked around. He didn't see or hear Mac. As he pulled on his pants, he looked around the house. "Hey, Mac. Are you here?"

No Mac. He shrugged, walked to the front door, opened it, and stepped onto the porch. "What a beautiful morning," he said, leaning on the railing, and taking a deep breath of the cool air.

John began to realize that he had become so caught up in the daily grind that he'd forgotten what was really important to him. He tried to remember the last time he'd just hung out in the mountains. Just then, he heard a faint whistling sound. The whistling got louder and louder. Sure enough, it was Mac, coming up the pathway, looking as happy as a clam at high tide.

"Top of the morning to you," Mac sang out. "How'd you sleep?"

"I think I slept great. I don't know, I was asleep."

"How about breakfast?" Mac asked, rolling his eyes at John's humor.

John was always hungry when he got up. In addition, he remembered how good dinner was. "I'm starving," John said as he looked down at his stomach and saw that he was far from starving. Mac could see that John was feeling more relaxed this morning. John also noticed how much more energetic and alive he felt.

****

"Breakfast was *fan-tastic*," John stated, dusting the crumbs off his lap.

"I'm glad you enjoyed it." As he put the dishes into the sink, Mac asked, "How'd you like to go for a walk? It's a beautiful morning. Maybe we can shake some of this food into our legs. The dishes can wait until we get back."

"Lead on," John answered.

Within a few minutes they were walking along a dirt path, surrounded by evergreens and wildflowers. As they started to head down a fork in the path that led to a small pond, Mac asked, "do you have any questions about the first five *Secrets*?"

"None that haven't been answered," John said. "There was a lot of information, but so far it all makes sense. I do wish I could have recorded it all."

"Not to worry," Mac commented, "Your inner mind stores memories of everything that has ever happened to you --everything you've ever read, learned or experienced. When you need any of this information trust it to be there and it will be.

"Are you ready to hear more?" Mac asked.

"Definitely," John stated. "I have all day." Mac smiled, knowing he didn't 'have all day'. He wanted to go play golf later.

Mac began. "*Secret 6* is *Do What Works For You*. It may be the easiest *Secret* to understand, but one of the least applied. To me, it is very literal. If you find something that works for you, do it. If something isn't working for you, do something else."

"But," John said, "How will you know when something isn't working?"

"By knowing what you want," Mac answered. "Remember, by knowing what you want, you will have a reference point to work toward. Once you're in touch with your goal, keep an eye on the actions you're taking. If they're not moving you toward what you want, change what you're doing.

"If golfers understood and embraced this *Secret,* they would stop trying to work on so many things at once, they would eliminate the belief that the golf swing is the answer to all their golfing problems, and they'd stop thinking about their swing on the golf course, because they'd see that doing those things wasn't helping them."

"Yes," John said, catching on quickly. "It seems like we would rather work harder and do more of something that isn't working, than just open our minds to another way."

"A teaching pro told me a story about a student who became very frustrated during a playing lesson. He asked him to stop trying to swing how he thought he *should* swing, and instead to do what was the most fun for him. He set up to the next ball and *wham!*, hit it longer and straighter than he'd hit a ball all day.

"'What'd you do differently?' he asked. After a few seconds, his student replied, 'I didn't take a practice swing.' He then continued by saying, 'I've never liked taking practice swings, and never hit the ball as well when I do'. 'Why have you continued to do them then?' 'I was told it was the right thing to do, so I figured eventually I'd *get it*', he said.

"Is that crazy or what? This golfer was told that the *right* thing to do was to take a practice swing. Even after repeatedly proving that it didn't work for him, he trusted the advice of someone else over his own knowledge of what was working for him.

"But Mac," John said, "If you don't listen to what the good players say, how will you know what to do?"

"Don't misunderstand me, I think it's very helpful to learn from other people, especially golf professionals. However, I don't think you should believe that something is *right*, until you make sure it's right for you.

"Golfers who believe that there is only one right way to swing and play golf, and that someone other than themselves has that knowledge, are setting themselves up for failure. By looking inside and deciding for myself, I am able to find the *one* way that works best for me."

"What do you mean by 'looking inside'?" John asked.

"Looking inside means asking myself useful questions and waiting for the answer that is right for me. For example, if I am on the fringe of the green, I could rely on a general rule of thumb, such as, if the grass isn't closely mowed, I will always chip.

"The way that I prefer to do it though is to hold the putter in one hand and the chipper in the other, get quiet inside, and wait for a signal. Within seconds I've always got some feeling as to which one is right."

They were just about at the pond. "Let's sit down for a minute." Mac asked, while pointing to a tree that had fallen at the edge of the water.

"What do you mean by *getting quiet inside*?" John asked as they sat.

"So glad you asked," Mac whispered, as if this was top secret information. "Getting quiet means silencing the voice in your head."

"What if I don't have a voice in my head?"

"We all talk to ourselves, even though we may not be aware of it, or call it a voice. For example, ask yourself how old you are." Mac gave John a few seconds to do it. How do you know you just asked yourself a question?"

John's eyes lit up. "I get it."

"When you quiet the voice in your head, you stop the conscious mind from interfering with the extraordinary abilities of the subconscious. Discovering that one of the components of my optimal golfing state of mind is to be quiet inside, has helped me drop several strokes off my scores."

"How do *you* get quiet inside?" John asked.

"The way I get quiet," Mac said, whispering at first, and then loudly exclaiming, "is by *doing* it. Just like I just change my outer voice, I change my inner voice -- its volume, tone, pitch, and so on.

"If you want to learn how to get quiet inside, the first thing you need to do is become aware that the voices exist. Next, learn how to change them by varying their components and seeing what happens. This is the time to make the voice louder; push it far away; bring it up close; garble it; make it very quiet and so on. Finally, the goal is to quiet the voice completely. You can experiment on the practice range with this."

"I like that. I'll try it next time I want my inner voice to disappear."

"Excellent! Are you ready to start back to the house now?"

"Ready and willing." John and Mac got up, both admiring the beauty of the morning sun on the water.

John felt especially satisfied. "I now have six *Secrets* ," he said.

"And the best is yet to come!" Mac enthusiastically replied.

Remember the Good Things

"*Secret 7*, Mac said taking a deep breath, "is *Remember the Good Things.* If we take the time to think about them, there are a lot of wonderful things to remember."

John agreed but then added half-jokingly, "And there are a lot of cruddy things to think about, too."

"Well, John, you think about those things and spiral toward them and I'll think about the good things and spiral upward. We'll see who gets their desires sooner!"

"I was just kidding. I plan on spiraling upward too."

"Good, because one of the fastest ways to spiral upward is to *remember the good things.* Remembering the good things places those images into your subconscious. For example, if you want to move in the direction of lower scores, you need to remember everything good you do while golfing.

"You mean, 'I had a good drive on 5', 'I mostly two-putted today'? Like that?" John asked.

"Yes and no. Yes, those are good things. And, no, I don't mean to remember, as if you were remembering the ingredients of a recipe; I mean to REMEMBER in the excited way you would remember sinking a hole-in-one -- I mean to wallow in all the good you do -- to remember the good things in every cell of my body." As Mac spoke, his voice got louder and his movements got more animated.

"It sounds simple doesn't it? Yet, what do most golfers do? They spend the majority of their golf time thinking about what they are doing wrong," Mac said, spiraling his index finger downward in the air, and making the sound of a bomb falling from the sky.

"How about you, John? Think back to the last time you were on the driving range. What were you thinking?"

"Well," he said, slowly while his brain busily scanned his past behavior on the golf course. He kept catching himself focusing on the *negatives*. Mac could see John's facial expression changing the more he thought.

"Most of my thoughts after swinging were about what I needed to change," John admitted.

"In other words, you thought about what you were doing wrong?"

"Ya, I'm afraid so."

"John, let's talk again about the average golfer on the driving range," Mac said, bending to pick up a stick from the side of the path.

Pretending it was a golf club, Mac swung. "Geez, I lifted by head," he scoffed. Mac swung again. "Aargh, I topped it." Mac swung a third time, even more determined. "Dang it, I swayed off the ball."

After a few more swings, with attendent explanations of what he'd done wrong, Mac frowned and dropped his head to his chest. "I can't hit my irons or my woods. I'll never be a good golfer."

John clapped in appreciation of the show and asked, "But, if I don't think about what I'm doing wrong, how will I ever be able to change it?"

"Never mind," John blurted, before Mac could start to answer, as he remembered *Secret 1* and *Secret 3*. John quickly realized that if he applied those *Secrets*, he would always know what he wanted his result to be *prior* to hitting a golf ball.

Mac continued to spell out *Secret 6*. "All you really need to do to prove how often golfers remember the bad over the good is eavesdrop on their conversations," Mac added. "I'd have played great if I hadn't three-putted those 17 greens," Mac exaggerated, imitating a golfer sitting in the coffee shop after his round.

"We could make it so much easier for ourselves if we would reward ourselves for the *good* things and leave the *bad* behind."

John nodded.

Mac, confident he'd made his point, threw away the stick and began to walk again.

"I've been living the *10 Secrets* now for over 20 years and, every now and then, I still catch myself spending time remembering how I messed something up or giving energy to what I don't want. The difference now is that the majority of my thoughts support the direction of higher self-esteem and possibilities."

Within five minutes, Mac's house was clearly in view. Another minute and they'd be there. The entire walk back John had been wondering whether he'd made a good decision when he threw his clubs into the lake. What if the *Secrets* could help him get his game back on track? His reflections were interrupted when Mac said, "Home again, home again . . . could I get you anything to drink or eat?"

"No thank you," John answered. "I'll just take a seat out here. But could you bring me my paper and pen so I could catch up on *Secret 6* and *7*?"

"Coming right up." After a few minutes Mac came out with a pitcher of water, two glasses, and the pen and paper.

John wrote the following notes:

SECRET 6 —
DO WHAT WORKS FOR YOU.

Keep in mind what I want
and notice if what I'm
doing is moving me closer
to it.

Look inside, get quiet and
decide for myself.

To get quiet, change the
components of the ~~voices~~
words in my head.

SECRET 7 ~
REMEMBER THE GOOD THINGS

Remember everything good
that I do! — To help me
SPIRAL towards what
I WANT.

EXPERIENCE the good
feelings over and over
again.

Secret 8

Make the Most of the Present

Mac started talking again as soon as he saw that John was finished writing. "*Secret 8*, is *Make the Most of the Present.* To me, this means to make the most of what I have *right now* -- not think of what's happened in the past -- not think of what I *could* have -- simply *be* with what *is* right now.

"Believe it or not, without changing anything else, most golfers would lower their scores, at least by a few strokes, by simply paying attention to this *Secret.* "

"How so?" John asked.

"Most golfers have better skills, right now, than they believe they have. Compare it to the process of learning to drive a car with a manual clutch. Do you remember all the separate steps you needed to learn in order to drive?"

After thinking about it for a minute, John replied, "Well, it's harder to remember than I thought because everything now it is so *automatic*. First, I put on my seatbelt. Then I put in the key and turn on the ignition. At about the same time I press down the brake and the clutch pedal. Then I shift." John chuckled. "It's taking me longer to say it than it takes me to do it."

"You've got the main idea," Mac stated. "At first, learning how to drive takes a bit of time, and conscious effort. Then we pass our driving test and get our driver's license."

"Around the time we receive our license, we trust that we know how to drive, and we begin to do all sorts of things while driving -- other than thinking about the mechanics of it. We look at other people, listen to cassettes, write down notes, and think about any multitude of things, even though we know better. Certainly, to do all these other things, we've learned to *trust* our subconscious ability to handle the habit of driving. That's the same process we need to use in our golf game."

"But," John asked, "How can you compare driving to golfing? Doesn't it take some people years to learn the skill of golfing?"

"Actually, the basic physical skills needed for a golf swing habit can be made into a habit in less than a month. Really . . . how hard is it to turn back and then forward?" Mac pantomimed a golf swing. "Your swing is a habit; my swing is a habit; and anyone who has been golfing more than 20 times, has a golf swing that's a habit."

"How can you say that golfers who hit the ball all over the place, right, left, low, and high, slicing and hooking, can have a golf swing that's a habit?" John questioned in disbelief.

"Prove it to yourself, John. Think about three people you've watched make a golf swing. If these three people stood behind a curtain so that all you could see was a shadow of each of them swinging, would you be able to distinguish one from the other? . . .Yes, of course you would."

"I see what you mean."

"Most golfers are inconsistent because they don't use their swing habit. They are stuck in *golfer's education class* and won't give themselves their golfing license. To make the most of your swing, you need to start to *trust* it -- similar to how you trusted your ability to drive after receiving your driver's license. But, noooooo!" Mac joked, "That's too easy.

"Many golfers say that their problem is their swing," Mac continued. "In the majority of cases, the biggest problem is that they're not making the most of their present swing."

"In fact," Mac elaborated, "I guarantee that a golfer will always play better allowing their subconscious to handle their current habit, as opposed to consciously thinking about their swing -- no matter how much their current habit produces inconsistent results."

"So," John questioned, "are you saying to just go out on the course and try to think of nothing?"

"No. On the course, I recommend playing *target golf.*"

"Target golf?" John asked.

"It's thinking about your target."

"That makes sense," John said, "because when you think about what you want, you tremendously increase your chances of achieving it."

"Exactly!" Mac cheered, standing up. "John, maybe you already play target golf. Would you like to find out?"

"Sure," John replied, following Mac's lead and getting up.

"OK John, pretend you're on your favorite golf course. Pick a particular hole on the course. Visualize your ball and the shot you are about to make -- something other than a putt. Pull out the appropriate club and take your set-up."

John was starting to feel more comfortable around Mac and was allowing himself to have more fun doing what Mac asked. He took his stance, looked out at an imaginary pin and then looked to Mac for further instructions.

"Start to take your swing and . . . " John started to swing. Keep my eyes on the ball, swing slowly, transfer my weight and follow through, he reminded himself.

"Stop," Mac shouted, as John had completed his takeaway and was about to start his forward swing. "What are you thinking *right now*?"

John felt a rush of heat in his face, "I don't want to say."

"I take it you weren't playing target golf," Mac said, smiling, as he sat down again. John remained standing.

"The way to hit a target is to think about it," Mac reiterated. "Since you can only think about one thing at a time, if you think about your golf swing while swinging on the golf course, you can't be thinking about your target. The irony is that many golfers actually get upset if they don't reach their target, even though they aren't thinking about it."

"John, start walking in that direction," Mac said, pointing toward a big pine tree. John thought the request was strange but had been around Mac long enough to trust him.

"Now," Mac continued, "start to notice how much knee bend you need, how long each of your steps are, how your hips move, and so on." After a few minutes, Mac added, "Now change how you walk. Walk with more knee bend and take longer steps." As John did, his walking changed and became less fluid. At first he felt self-conscious, but soon he started to have fun with the exercise by lifting his arms up and down in an ape-like fashion. He laughed at himself as he stopped by the far side of the porch.

Mac was smiling, then suddenly asked with all seriousness, "John, why didn't you walk over to the pine tree?"

John said, somewhat defensively, "I was thinking about changing my walking, not the pine tree."

"There, you've proved my point."

"What point is that?"

"You proved that you <u>can't</u> think about your target, and your physical swing mechanics at the same time. In this case, your target was the tree and your swing mechanics was your walking." Mac could see that John now understood.

"Isn't what you just did here a familiar scene for many golfers on the golf course?" Mac asked, wanting to drive the point home. "They get up to their ball, think about where they need to direct their shot, then promptly forget about it and start thinking about the physical mechanics of their swing."

John imagined what it'd be like to play target golf. "Do you even play target golf when the proverbial 'wheels are falling off' your game?"

"*Especially* then," Mac replied. "Many times the 'wheels fall off' because there is too much conscious interference. Keeping your mind on the target inhibits your ability to consciously interfere with your swing. As a side note, it is possible, however," Mac added, "to consciously interfere with your swing by *trying* to hit to a target. The key word is *try*. *Trying* is being conscious. Therefore, as much as possible, I recommend that you don't *try* to do things, rather, just *do* them."

"But how do I just *do* it?" John said.

"Oh, that million dollar question again. The answer is, just pretend that you can.

"And, in relation to target golf, each of us has one way to connect with the target that will work best for us. Some people *see* the target, others get a *feel* for the target, while others may get a sense of rhythm, balance, or *sound* that mentally connects them to it. Experiment with each to find out which way will work best for you. It's a great time to use your imagination."

"That sounds good in concept," John said, "but how would I play target golf to the middle of a wide open fairway where I wouldn't have a specific target?"

"You just pick the spot you want to hit to and *imagine* any target you want at that spot. Why do you think that many golfers seem to hit some of their most solid shots out of the trees? Because they have to imagine the path they want the ball to take and as they swing, they are thinking about that path. In essence -- target golf. Of course, when the ball is back in the fairway they start thinking about their swing again and hit it back into the hazard," Mac teased.

"Well, it won't happen to me," John exclaimed.

"Then we're ready to go on to the next *Secret*," Mac said, sensing John may be ready to play golf again.

"OK, give me one or two minutes and I'll be all yours," John said. He picked up the paper and pencil and wrote:

Secret 8 —

MAKE THE MOST OF THE PRESENT

Use what I have right <u>now</u>.

To learn:

1st-- learn the skill (consciously). Once done, trust my abilities. (i.e. get driver's license, get golfer's license)

2nd-- learn to <u>use</u> the skill. Trust the subconscious to adjust (i.e. drive the car, play golf)

FOR GOLF:

On the golf course, think only about the target— use my imagination.

When John was done writing, Mac said, "Great day for a game of golf," looking for a reaction out of the corner of his eye. "I have my golf clubs in the house, and my own personal course. How about it?"

"Sure," John said hesitantly, filled with doubt. He decided to give it a go anyway.

Change What You Want to Change

The fairways on Mac's course were very narrow openings amidst very tall trees. Instead of grass, there was dirt and pine needles. The pins had been made out of long sticks and sail cloth. And the holes, although three par in distance, were five par in challenge.

Mac's course had 5 local rules:

1. Create a powerful state of mind *prior* to swinging.
2. Trust your swing (pretend it's perfect the way it is).
3. Create powerful target images to have *while* swinging.
4. Remember everything good that happens.
5. Do anything that makes playing more fun.

It took them about an hour to play the 6-hole course. John had some great shots, and some not-so-great. Either way, he had never had as much fun playing golf. He gave a lot of credit to Mac and his local rules.

During the round, Mac and John had started an unspoken challenge to see which one could get the most outrageous. Creating a powerful state of mind included placing their arms above their head in victory signs and doing routines of everything they'd seen sports celebrities do when psyched.

Some of their target images were quite unique. They included famous people, animals, and rainbows, in an array of colors. For fun, they teed up balls on pine cones, and swung any way that was the most fun for them. After each shot, they'd each go into a speech about everything good about their shot and the useful things they'd been thinking.

****

When they returned to the house, Mac refilled the pitcher with water and ice, and they sat on the porch reminiscing about their favorite shots. The recent round with John had increased Mac's desire to play 9-holes later at a local course down the mountain.

"Thanks," John said repeatedly, "that was wonderful. I had forgotten how much fun golfing could be. But," John stated, "I would never act like that on a real golf course."

"I agree," Mac said, "I doubt it would be considered good golf etiquette."

"So, how do you have as much fun as we just did while still maintaining course manners?" John asked.

"For someone like me, who feels more powerful when I am a bit outrageous, I do it inside my head," Mac answered. "As you can see by watching many of the professionals, great golf can be played in a quiet way, too. As a matter of fact, the optimal state of mind for many golfers is a more centered and peaceful one. The key is to do what comes naturally to you."

"Um-huh," John nodded.

"Are you ready to hear about *Secret 9* now?" Mac asked.

"You bet," John enthusiastically responded, still pumped up from golfing.

"*Secret 9* is *Change What You Want to Change.* This means that anything you've learned, you can change. All you need to do to change is think about what you want until the change is in your subconscious.

"The keys are to think about one thing at a time, to give yourself adequate time to make the change, and to have a way to know when you'll be done making the change.

"There are a few general rules of thumb that I've used to let me know I'm done developing a new habit. The one I used most often," Mac said, "was to practice my desired change for 21-days in a row, 60 repetitions a day. I usually did two sets of 30 repetitions, but sometimes I did all 60 at once."

"Why 21-days?" John asked.

"According to neuroscientists, 21-days is the incubation period needed for the brain to 'hatch' a new habit."

"Twenty-one days sounds like an awful long time," John moaned.

"At first it did to me, too," Mac replied, "but then I relived the years I'd spent working on my swing without success. By comparison, 21-days seemed like a snap. I especially recommend using 21-day plans for pre-swing changes," Mac added.

"What part of the swing do you consider the pre-swing?" John asked.

"The pre-swing or physical set-up, includes everything that you physically do while addressing the ball prior to actually swinging. This includes the grip, alignment, stance, posture, and so on.

"All you need to do to develop the perfect pre-swing is place your body into the desired position and count it as one repetition. Then you stand up, shake your body out," Mac said, demonstrating what it'd be like, "and do it again."

"Are you saying that you don't have to ever hit a ball?" John asked.

"Precisely," Mac said. "You can easily practice at home without any balls."

"So, that's how I'd learn the pre-swing. What about the swing motion?" John asked.

"For that, I use something I call the *programming process*. It allows me to make any change quickly and easily."

"I'm all ears," John said, pointing to the side of his head.

"Each repetition of the *programming process* consists of five easy steps," Mac said, still smiling at John's comment:

1. Vividly imagine achieving your desired change perfectly.
2. Take a slow motion swing, without a ball, doing your change perfectly (a 10 on a scale of 1 to 10).
3. Swing at regular speed, *noticing* how close you came to your perfect 10.
4. Rate how close you came to your desired change on a scale of 1 to 10.
5.   a. If it is a 10, get excited about what a great job you did and repeat the process beginning at step three.

      b. If it's <u>not</u> a 10, think about what would need to be different to make it a 10 and repeat the process beginning at step one.

"To put it simply, to make any swing change, all you do is show your brain what you want, take a swing and see how close you come. If you don't do it perfectly while swinging, then show your brain what you want again, swing and see how close you came again. You simply do this process over and over again until you feel you are a 10."

"I might have a hard time with that because I don't like to give myself a 10 on anything since I know I can always do better," John stated.

"I understand what you're saying. However, to change your swing motion habit, you first need to know specifically what your desired change is. If you don't, your brain won't have a goal. Since you need to know your desired change, you should be able to know when it's perfect. You either do it perfectly or you don't."

"And, it still isn't necessary to hit a ball?" John asked.

"I'm glad you noticed that John. Yes, just like when working on the pre-swing, it isn't necessary to hit balls. In fact, sometimes hitting balls will even detract from your practice session because it adds unnecessary pressure.

"Many people start to care about where the ball goes instead of keeping their mind tracking on whether or not they are moving toward what they want. And because they are being conscious about their swing, odds are they won't hit the ball very well anyway."

"Actually, practicing swing changes at home sound great to me," John said. "It'll be easier to find the time without having to pack up and go to the course."

"And, at home," Mac added, "You can practice one of two ways. You can either:

1. Physically do the desired position or motion.
2. Or, mentally imagine the desired position or motion.

"Since the brain records a *real* shot exactly the same as a *vividly* imagined one, you can even practice while laying in bed, showering, sitting at stoplights or waiting in lines.

"Geez, I didn't know that," John stated.

"The last key is to learn to celebrate when you have completed a change, and give yourself permission to BE DONE. Again, golf is a great example of how the opposite occurs. Because of how golf is normally taught, I think that the idea of being done is one of the hardest, and most rewarding, things you can do."

"I believe you."

"In conclusion," Mac said definitively, "don't do what I used to do. Don't think about your swing change while on the golf course. Golf instruction often gets a bum rap because many golfers get worse before they get better when taking lessons."

"I'm living proof," John interjected.

"Well, I know it's not usually fun when it happens," Mac sympathized, "but it doesn't have to be the case. For example, let's pretend you are a golfer who has just taken a lesson and found out what you need to do to improve. After practicing for a few days, you get onto the golf course. You now understand that there is a better way to swing than what you've been doing so you try (consciously) to use your new information. Unfortunately, the new information is not yet in your subconscious.

"Consciously thinking about your new swing habit before it is in your subconscious produces a struggling, frustrated golfer who blames lessons for messing his game up. Does that make sense?" Mac asked.

"I think so," John said.

"Well, if you don't know for sure . . . who does?" Mac teased. They both smiled.

"We're at a good stopping point again," Mac commented. "Is there anything I could get, or do, for you?"

"I'm doing just fine, thanks," John answered, marveling at Mac's hospitality. "I think I'll just get up, move around a bit, and make a few more notes."

"OK, I'll be out in a minute," Mac said, as he walked back into the house.

This is what John wrote:

SECRET 9 ~
CHANGE WHAT YOU WANT TO CHANGE

To change any habit –

Practice 1 change at a time until it is in my subconscious.

Rule of thumb – 21 days in a row

FOR GOLF

PROGRAMMING PROCESS:

1. Imagine the change I want to make – vividly.
2. Do the change in slow motion without a ball.
3. Swing at regular speed (with or without a ball) keeping my mind on my desired change & noticing how close I come to it.
4. Rate how close on a scale of 1 to 10.
5. If it's great, repeat at step 3. If not, repeat at #1.

Practicing swing changes works equally well at home as it does on the range. It can be done physically or by vividly imagining.
Allow myself to be done & Celebrate!

Secret 10

Have Fun

About 10 minutes later, Mac came out with a tray full of snacks. "On second thought," John said, looking at the sandwiches, "I *am* a bit hungry."

****

After they'd demolished all the edibles, John said, "I think we did a *10* on that food." They both laughed.

Mac picked up the empty tray and whisked it back into the kitchen. A couple of minutes later, he rejoined John.

"And now for the moment of truth," Mac said, smiling. "You journeyed up here seeking to find a way to be happier and the time has come. Time for the tenth and final *Secret*. To live happily ever after, all you need to do is, *Have Fun,*" Mac said definitively.

John had a smirk on his face as he said, "that's all you do, huh?"

"John, I remember reading this *Secret* on the golf course that late night many moons ago and thinking exactly the same thing," Mac responded. "But I've grown to realize the depth of its simplicity."

"There must be a lot more to having fun than I've thought about," John said, lifting his eyebrows.

"Well, ponder the concept," Mac said. "When you're having fun, you feel better about yourself. When you feel good about yourself, you have a powerful state of mind. When you have a powerful state of mind, you are most likely to produce desirable results."

John nodded in acknowledgement. It was certainly a logical progression, as was all of Murphy's advice.

"Many people believe in working hard so they can have fun *later,* or they let fun be a reward only when they do *well.* Why not find a way to enjoy everything now?" Mac asked. "That means your behavior, your feelings, your golf shots and so on. When we make things fun, we do more of them and more often. The opposite is also true. For example, why don't golfers practice more often?"

"Because it's boring and it's work," John answered.

"Yes, that's what most golfers associate with practice," Mac agreed. "But if we know that we need to practice to improve, then why not make practice fun?"

"OK, but what if your practice shots are fun and then you get on the course and everything turns sour?" John questioned.

"It's no different than practice, John," Mac replied. "All you need to do is find something good about what is happening. Even the worst shot can be a *friend*, if you find something good about it.

"Even those times when I can't see much good about a shot, I find something that I can learn from it,. The fact that I can learn from it is something good to me.

"There is a less frivolous side to this as well," Mac added. "If there is something that you don't like and you try to prevent it, then you are giving it energy. And when we give things energy, we what? . . ."

"We get more of it," John responded.

"Right," Mac agreed. "Therefore, for golfing success, I suggest you find a way to enjoy everything you do and feel during practice and play. Decide to find a way to have fun even when you're not playing well and, I guarantee you, you will not only become a better golfer, but you'll have the time of your life doing it!"

"You mean, I can actually leave the course feeling better about myself?" John asked, poking fun at his past behavior.

"You got it!" Mac said, giving John a *high-five*. Then he grabbed a nearby stick and wrote this in the dirt in front of John:

PART 3:

MOVING FORWARD

Playtime

It was mid-afternoon. "Well," Mac said, "that's what the *10 Secrets* mean to me."

"Pretty powerful stuff," John replied.

"Let me show you what happens if you outline them."

John took out the sheet listing the 10 *Secrets*. Within a few seconds, Mac penciled in what it looked like:

The 10 Secrets

Know What You Want

Believe What Supports You

Give Energy To What You Want

Feel Like You're Going to Succeed

Trust Yourself

Do What Works For You

Remember the Good Things

Make the Most of the Present

Change What You Want to Change

Have Fun

John smiled. "I hadn't noticed that."

"You see John," Mac said, "the *Secrets* will always help you move toward what you want."

"Mac, you make it all sound so *easy*. Are you able to go out and break par anytime you want?"

"That would be great, and I don't rule it out as a possibility," Mac answered with a grin. "However, while the techniques are easy, in and of themselves, making changes can take time. Even while using the *10 Secrets*, sometimes the downhill spiral can *temporarily* get the upper hand. In other words, I still get frustrated, I still have things that bother me, and I still have powerless states of mind. The difference now is that I can quickly get back on track.

"What I recommend is often seen as a paradox. On the one hand, remind yourself that it's possible to change immediately. On the other hand, know that sometimes it takes time to make changes permanent. At times, you may feel like you're getting worse before you get better.

"Personally, I've learned the hard way, and the easy way, that using the 10 Secrets is the quickest and easiest way to make the lasting, long-term changes I want. While I may not shoot a 69 everytime I play, I know that I am continually improving in the overall game."

John looked down for a moment and then looked at Mac and said, "I can't begin to thank you enough. I have learned more than I can tell you. I think I've found my missing link, and perhaps most amazingly, I'm excited about playing golf again."

"I thank *you*," Mac said. "The pleasure was mine! I've enjoyed the company. And, talking about the *Secrets* is fun for me. Of course, what's even more fun is putting the information to use. So . . . why don't you consider salvaging those clubs?

Mac continued. "Doing, being, and having anything you want in life is simple. All you need is to know what you want and imagine that you have it. Then, believe what supports you, keep thinking only of what you want and feel like you're going to succeed. Take action and trust yourself and the limitless personal power you have to adapt for the better. Do more of what works for you and stop doing what doesn't. Remember everything good you do. And, make the most of what you have in the present, but know that you can change what you want to change."

"And above all," John broke in, "have fun at all times." They both laughed.

"That's perfect! In addition, John, as you work with the *Secrets*, please feel free to share with others what we've discussed," Mac offered, hoping John would spread the word. "One of the beneficial things about the *10 Secrets* is that they pertain to all people, no matter their age or achievement in life.

"Every time you share it, not only do I think you'll be helping others, you'll also get closer to making the *Secrets* habits in your subconscious. If you use this information for your golf game, just think what a great role model you'll be. Other golfers will ask you what has made such a difference in your game, and you can share the *Secrets* with them. Like you, what many of them have been doing probably hasn't been working."

John looked up and thought about what Mac had said. He liked the idea and wondered how he could share the information and make it fun. He wanted to think more about that later. Right now, he couldn't wait to get back to tell his wife and friends what had happened on the mountaintop.

****

John raised his hand in salute and goodbye. As he began heading down the mountain, he heard Mac gathering up his clubs so that he could squeeze in a few more holes before dark.

****

A week later, John picked up the phone in his living room and was surprised by Mac's voice.

"Just called to say hi. How's everything going?" Mac asked.

"Much better. They'd missed me at work and my wife was a little worried, but I had a good excuse. I told her I had just spent two days with the *Golf God* . . .

the end

of the Beginning

NOTES

Categorize your feelings

[Empowering]:
~~happiness~~
confidence
creativity
decisiveness
serenity
centeredness

weakening
fear, anger, confusion, tiredness
frustration.

NOTES

State of mind as a menu
when you feel powerful
Menu might list these choices:
- you will connect the ball solidly
  and to land five yards left of
  target.
- you will hit the low with distance
  etc.

To control the state of mind you want
the fastest and easiest way to change
what your body is doing:
- facial expression
- breathing
- stance
- movement
What we do with our body sends
direct messages to our brain.

Head & eyes up
shoulders back
Slight Smile
Breathing easy & relaxed
walking - even paced.

NOTES

NOTES

NOTES

Recommendations for Further Study

Advanced Psycho-Cybernetics and Psychofeedback, Paul Thomas, (book)

Change Your Mind and Keep the Change, Dr. Connirae and Steve Andreas, (book)

Creative Dreaming, Patricia Garfield, (book)

Creative Visualization, Shakti Gawain, (book)

Five Days to Golfing Excellence, Chuck Hogan (book)

Frogs Into Princes, Richard Bandler and John Grinder, (book)

Golf in the Kingdom, Michael Murphy, (book)

Golfer's Profile System, Chuck Hogan and Performax, (Self-Administered Personal Analysis)

How to Become a Complete Golfer, Bob Toski and Jim Flick, (book for ball flight concepts)

How to Live and Be Free Through Psycho-Cybernetics, Dr. Maxwell Maltz and Charles Schreiber, (book and cassettes)

Inner Game of Golf, Tim Gallwey, (book)

Living in the Light, Shakti Gawain, (book)

Love, Sex, and Communication, Phil Laut and Jeanne Miller, (book)

Magical Child, Joseph Chilton Pearce, (book)

Mind-Shapes; Inside-Out; and Images Are M.E., Susan Davis and Dale Van Dalsem, (cassettes)

NICE SHOT, Chuck Hogan, (video)

Personal Power, Anthony Robbins, (30-day cassette program)

Psycho-Cybernetics, Dr. Maxwell Maltz, (book)

Stretching, Bob Anderson, (book)
Sybervision Muscle Memory Programming, Steven
    DeVore and Dr. Gregory DeVore, (book)
The 10 Basics, Gene Littler, (video)
Twelve Means to Lower Scores, Chuck Hogan,
    (cassettes)
Unlimited Power, Anthony Robbins, (book)
Using Your Brain For a Change, Richard Bandler,
    (book)
You Can Have it All, Arnold Patent, (book)
You Can Heal Your Life, Louise Hay, (book)
You'll See It When You Believe It, Dr. Wayne Dyer,
    (book)
Your Fondest Dream, Jim Leonard, (book)

Most of the products above are available at your favorite
bookseller or can be ordered from:

ON TARGET Enterprises
P.O. Box 163438
Sacramento, CA 95816-9438

Toll-free **(800) 743-4-FUN**

ON TARGET
Enterprises

ON TARGET Enterprises is dedicated to improving the quality of people's lives.

Via exciting, fun and informative presentations, seminars and products, it is our goal to assist people in achieving their desired level of success and happiness.

By synthesizing years of research and practical application with the world's most advanced self-improvement techniques, we bring our clients information on the cutting edge of the self-development field. The results -- ON TARGET programs and presentations use the most effective and specialized concepts, technologies and strategies to facilitate the move through limitations toward the achievement of each individual's success.

By combining education with fun and humor, we believe that men and women of all ages can clarify their knowledge of what makes them happy, create plans, take precise actions, and achieve success in a way far easier than ever imagined.

While the techniques we utilize are useful in all parts of life, we have chosen golf as the primary vehicle through which we share these "life-improvement" strategies.

For more information, a schedule of upcoming seminars and schools, or for a list of available products, contact:

ON TARGET Enterprises
P.O. Box 163438
Sacramento, CA 95816-9438

Toll-free **(800) 743-4-FUN**